^{THE} bread breakthrough

EASY RECIPES • DOUGH KNEADS ITSELF

by **NANCY BAGGETT**

author of *Kneadlessly Simple: Fabulous, Fuss-Free, No-Knead Breads*

WILEY

JOHN WILEY & SONS, INC.

Published by John Wiley & Sons, Inc., Hoboken, New Jersey
Published simultaneously in Canada

For general information on our other products and services or for technical support, please contact our Customer Care Department within the United States at (800)
762–2974, outside the United States at (317) 572–3993 or fax (317) 572–4002.

Wiley also publishes its books in a variety of electronic formats. Some content that ap-
pears in print may not be available in electronic books. For more information about Wiley
products, visit our web site at www.wiley.com.

Library of Congress Cataloging-in-Publication Data

ISBN: 978-0-470-48558-3

Printed in the United States of America

10   9   8   7   6   5   4   3   2

Kneadlessly Simple—The Bread Breakthrough Brought to You by Fleischmann's® Yeast

Now you can bake bread reliably and easily with absolutely no kneading and little kitchen mess! The secret is a slow, cold-rise method, which not only lets the yeast slowly produce full, satisfying flavor, but amazing as it sounds, also gives the dough time to naturally knead itself! The Kneadlessly Simple method involves easy, reliable steps explained in a way that anyone can understand. Best of all the technique calls for minimal, economical ingredients often mixed in one bowl with one spoon.

A PROVEN TECHNIQUE ANYONE CAN DO

- No risk in killing the yeast with water that is too hot—all recipes use ice water.
- NO kneading! The dough naturally kneads itself.
- A long slow rise gives you a broad range of time between preparation and baking which means you can work the bread-making process into YOUR schedule!
- YOU know and control the ingredients (and can pronounce each one!).
- Great homemade taste and texture without the bakery price! A slow rise develops full, satisfying flavor.
- This is truly yeast baking demystified! Guaranteed every time.

Nancy Baggett, Creator of the Kneadlessly Simple technique

Nancy Baggett loved serving fresh, fragrant bread from her oven—but found it difficult to find time to prepare her mother's yeast recipes. The Kneadlessly Simple technique is the result of her experimentation with a no-knead, slow-rise method that incorporated (yet simplified) techniques used by artisan bakers. Nancy is a baking expert, food journalist and bestselling cookbook author. She contributes to *Eating Well*, the *Washington Post*, and many other leading food magazines and newspapers. Nancy has appeared on *Good Morning America*, *Today*, *The Early Show*, the Discovery Channel, the Food Network, the History Channel, and other networks.

TRULY UNBELIEVABLY EASY AND FOOLPROOF

Don't be concerned by the length of the recipes in this book! You may think the recipes look long or complicated. But not so. The step-by-step instructions help guide you easily through the entire process of each exciting recipe. All the recipes use the same basic proven four steps:

1. Mix dough ingredients using ice water to make a stiff dough.

2. **FIRST RISE:** Let dough rise in a covered bowl on the counter for a long, cool rise. Or if more convenient, refrigerate the dough a while, then let sit on a counter for the long first rise. (Never skip the countertop rise.)

3. **SECOND RISE:** Add any additional ingredients; place dough in pan and let rise in the refrigerator or on the counter or a combination of both until dough doubles.

4. Bake in preheated oven.

FULL-TIME PROFESSIONAL CUSTOMER SUPPORT

Only Fleischmann's Yeast has a full-time, trained professional staff to help bakers at all levels of experience bake their best. Our consumer support staff is ready to assist you with product and baking advice at 1-800-777-4959. Our www.breadworld.com Web site also provides both helpful hints and a wide range of appealing baked good recipes.

TIPS TO MAKE YOUR HOMEMADE BAKING EXPERIENCE THE BEST IT CAN BE

- Always check the yeast expiration date before starting any yeast recipe.

- For best results, use an instant-read thermometer to test for doneness.

- Following a low-salt diet? Salt is an essential ingredient in yeast baking and cannot be omitted without significantly altering the quality of the bread.

- Flour is the key ingredient in bread, so the right measurement is very important. See tips for measuring flour on page 43.

- Baked goods are best eaten within 24 hours of baking (remember, home-baked yeast recipes contain no preservatives).

- Don't store baked bread in the refrigerator—it will become stale more quickly. See details for storing bread on page 45.

- Baked products can easily be frozen.

For additional tips on the Kneadlessly Simply method, go to page 43.

contents

While the recipes specify Fleischmann's RapidRise™ Yeast, all recipes in this book can also be made with Fleischmann's Bread Machine and Fleischmann's Instant (Brick-Pack) Yeast. Using yeast other than those listed above is not recommended.

easy
oat bread

KS QUOTIENT — Super Easy: A minimum of fuss-free, easily mixed ingredients. No hand-shaping.

Oats always seem to have a comforting, low-key flavor, and this bread does, too. The straightforward, easy recipe can be made with either honey or molasses and produces two homey, nice-to-have-on-hand loaves. (Stash one in the freezer for later use.)

The honey version is slightly sweeter and lighter in color; the molasses version, tastes—surprise!—of molasses, though it doesn't come on strong. Attractively flecked with bits of oats, the loaves are slightly soft and make excellent toast and sandwich bread.

Yield: 2 medium loaves, about 12 slices each

5½ cups (27.5 ounces) unbleached all-purpose white flour or unbleached white bread flour, plus more as needed

1 cup old-fashioned rolled oats or quick-cooking (not instant) oats, plus 4 tablespoons for garnish

3 tablespoons granulated sugar

Scant 2¾ teaspoons table salt

1 teaspoon Fleischmann's RapidRise Yeast

¼ cup clover honey or light (mild) molasses

¼ cup corn oil or other flavorless vegetable oil, plus extra for coating dough top and baking pans

2¼ cups plus 2 tablespoons ice water, plus more if needed

FIRST RISE: In a very large bowl, thoroughly stir together the flour, oats, sugar, salt, and yeast. In a medium bowl or measuring cup, thoroughly whisk the honey (or molasses) and oil into the water. Thoroughly stir the water mixture into the larger bowl, scraping down the sides until the ingredients are thoroughly blended. If the mixture is too dry to incorporate all the flour, a bit at a time, stir in just enough more water to blend the ingredients; don't over-moisten, as the dough should be stiff. Brush or spray the top with oil. Cover the bowl with plastic wrap. For best flavor or convenience, you can refrigerate the dough for 3 to 10 hours. Then let rise at cool room temperature for 12 to 18 hours; if convenient, vigorously stir once during the rise.

SECOND RISE: Vigorously stir the dough. If necessary, stir in enough more flour to yield a hard-to-stir consistency. Generously oil two $8^1\!/_2 \times 4^1\!/_2$-inch loaf pans. Sprinkle a tablespoon of oats in each; tip the pans back and forth to spread the oats over the bottom and sides. Use well oiled kitchen shears or a serrated knife to cut the dough into 2 equal portions. Put the portions in the pans. Brush or spray the tops with oil. Press and smooth the dough evenly into the pans with an oiled rubber spatula or fingertips. Sprinkle a tablespoon of oats over each loaf; press down to imbed. Make a $^1\!/_2$-inch-deep slash lengthwise down the center of each loaf using oiled kitchen shears or a serrated knife. Tightly cover the pans with nonstick spray-coated plastic wrap.

LET RISE USING ANY OF THESE METHODS: For a 2- to 3-hour regular rise, let stand at warm room temperature; for a 45-minute to 2-hour accelerated rise, let stand in a turned-off microwave along with 1 cup of boiling-hot water; or for an extended rise, refrigerate, covered, for 4 to 24 hours, then set out at room temperature. Continue the rise until the dough nears the plastic. Remove it and continue until the dough extends $^1\!/_2$ inch above the pan rims.

BAKING PRELIMINARIES: 15 minutes before baking time, place a rack in the lower third of the oven; preheat to 375°F.

BAKING: Bake on the lower rack for 50 to 60 minutes, until the tops are well browned. Cover the tops with foil. Then bake for 10 to 15 minutes more, until a skewer inserted in the thickest part comes out with just a few particles clinging to the bottom

portion (or until the center registers 208° to 210°F on an instant-read thermometer). Bake for 5 minutes longer to be sure the centers are done. Let cool in the pans on a wire rack for 15 minutes. Turn out the loaves onto racks and cool thoroughly.

SERVING AND STORING: Cool thoroughly before slicing or storing. Best served toasted. Store airtight in plastic or aluminum foil. The bread will keep at room temperature for 3 days, and may be frozen, airtight, for up to 2 months.

cheddar and chiles bread

KS QUOTIENT— Super Easy: A minimum of fuss-free, easily mixed ingredients. No hand-shaping.

The Hispanic influence on American culture over the past decades has been pervasive and shows up not only in the popularity of Mexican and Tex-Mex fare, but also in the widespread availability of ingredients like assorted chiles. Once found only in ethnic communities and markets, green chiles turn up in everything from soups and quiches to corn casseroles and both quick and yeast breads. (If you aren't familiar with green chiles, note that they are just slightly piquant; they are not the same as jalapeños.)

This is a delightfuly savory bread, particularly if a top-quality white cheddar is used. The loaf is shot through with cheese and bits of green chiles, and the crust is golden brown. It is great with chili, hearty, full-bodied soups, and bean dishes; it also makes an unusual but very appealing sandwich bread.

For a different look and milder taste, prepare the equally easy cheddar and pimiento variation provided at the end of the recipe.

Yield: 1 large loaf, 12 to 14 slices

3½ cups (17.5 ounces) unbleached white bread flour, plus more as needed

1 tablespoon granulated sugar

1½ teaspoons table salt

1 teaspoon Fleischmann's RapidRise Yeast

2 tablespoons corn oil, canola oil, or other flavorless vegetable oil, plus extra for coating dough top and baking pan

1⅔ cups ice water, plus more if needed

8 ounces (3 lightly packed cups) coarsely grated very sharp cheddar cheese, preferably white cheddar

½ cup very well-drained and patted dry chopped canned green chiles

FIRST RISE: In a large bowl, thoroughly stir together the flour, sugar, salt, and yeast. In another bowl or measuring cup, whisk the oil into the water. Thoroughly stir the mixture into the bowl with the flour, scraping down the sides until the ingredients are thoroughly blended. If the mixture is too dry to incorporate all the flour, a bit at a time, stir in just enough more ice water to blend the ingredients; don't over-moisten, as the dough should be stiff. If necessary, stir in enough more flour to stiffen it. Brush or spray the top with oil. Cover the bowl with plastic wrap. If desired, for best flavor or for convenience, you can refrigerate the dough for 3 to 10 hours. Then let rise at cool room temperature for 15 to 20 hours. If convenient, stir the dough once partway through the rise.

SECOND RISE: Vigorously stir the dough, gradually sprinkling over and incorporating the cheese and chiles. Fold them in very thoroughly to ensure they are evenly distributed. If necessary, thoroughly stir in enough more flour to yield a very stiff dough. Using a well-oiled rubber spatula, fold the dough in towards the center, working all the way around the bowl. Invert the dough into a well-greased 9 × 5-inch loaf pan. Evenly brush or spray the dough top with oil. Using well-oiled kitchen shears or a serrated knife, make a ¼-inch-deep slash lengthwise down the center of the loaf. Cover the pan with nonstick spray-coated plastic wrap.

LET RISE USING ANY OF THESE METHODS: For a 1½- to 2½-hour regular rise, let stand at warm room temperature; for a 1- to 2-hour accelerated rise, let stand in a turned-off microwave along with 1 cup of boiling-hot water; or for an extended rise, refrigerate for 4 to 24 hours, then set out at room temperature. Continue the rise until the dough nears the plastic. Remove it and continue until the dough reaches ½ inch above the pan rim.

BAKING PRELIMINARIES: 15 minutes before baking time, place a rack in the lower third of the oven; preheat to 425°F.

BAKING: Reduce the heat to 400°F. Bake for 30 to 40 minutes, unti the top is nicely browned; cover the top with foil as needed Continue baking for 20 to 30 minutes longer, or until a skewe inserted in the thickest part comes out with just a few particle clinging to the bottom (or until the center registers 204° to 206° on an instant-read thermometer). Then bake for 5 minutes mor to be sure the center is done. Cool in the pan on a wire rack for 1 minutes. Turn out the loaf onto the rack; cool thoroughly.

SERVING AND STORING: Cool thoroughly before slicing or storing. Stor airtight in plastic or aluminum foil. The bread will keep at roon temperature for 2 to 3 days, and may be frozen, airtight, for up t 2 months.

VARIATION CHEDDAR AND PIMIENTO BREAD—Omit the gree chiles and substitute an equal amount of well-drained and patte dry chopped jarred pimientos. Otherwise proceed exactly a directed.

going with the grain bread kit

This recipe enables you to prepare an appealing jar of bread mix to give a friend, relative, or anyone on your gift list. (Make up an extra jar, so you can easily treat yourself once in a while.) Even a novice baker can turn out this crusty, attractive loaf without muss or fuss and no ingredients other than water and a little vegetable oil. The big, rustic, versatile loaf has a mild yet addictive grain flavor and a light, springy, slightly holey crumb. It smells and tastes like an artisan bread, yet requires no artisan skills.

The flavor comes from the subtle blending of four grains, including some brown rice flour, and three seeds, including flax seed. These ingredients are not likely to be on hand in your cupboard, but are usually stocked in the gluten-free baking sections of health food stores, as well as in some large supermarkets.

Alternatively, prepare your own brown rice flour by grinding uncooked brown rice to a powder using a blender or clean coffee mill. (Measure out the ¼ cup after the flour is ground.) Regular long-grain brown rice will do, but if you can find it, brown basmati rice delivers the sweetest flavor. In a pinch, omit the flax seed from the recipe and add an extra 2 teaspoons each of the sesame and poppy seeds. The bread flavor will not be quite as irresistible, but will still be very good.

Yield: 1 quart of mix, yielding 1 large loaf

3 cups (15 ounces) unbleached white bread flour

¼ cup (1.25 ounces) whole wheat flour

¼ cup brown rice flour

2 tablespoons rolled oats or quick-cooking (not instant) oats

2½ tablespoons granulated sugar

1½ teaspoons table salt

1½ tablespoons *each* sesame seeds, poppy seeds, and flax seed, mixed together

2 tablespoons cornmeal, preferably yellow

1 envelope Fleischmann's RapidRise Yeast

Set out a completely dry clear glass or transparent plastic 1-quart or 1-liter jar, along with its lid. Set out a square of heavy-duty aluminum foil to use as a funnel. (Or use a funnel, if you have one.)

Place the white flour on the foil, then use the foil as a funnel to add the flour to the jar. Rap the jar on the counter to even and compact the layer. Thoroughly stir together the whole wheat flour, brown rice flour, oats, sugar, salt, and all but 1½ tablespoons of the seed mixture on the foil. Add to the jar; rap it again to even the layer. Put the remaining seeds and the cornmeal in a small plastic bag; close tightly. Push the bag and the yeast envelope into the neck of the jar. If it will be shipped, push crumpled wax paper into any extra space at the top. Attach a sheet or card with the instructions for making the bread to the jar.

STORAGE: The unopened mix will keep for up to 1½ months unrefrigerated, 3 months refrigerated.

Don't forget to give the following recipe along with your gift:

GOING WITH THE GRAIN BREAD RECIPE (USING MIX)

Along with ice water and vegetable oil, this kit makes a crusty-topped artisan-style loaf with a slight crunch and light, enticing flavor and aroma of grain. Great for eating warm or cooled, slathered with butter, for toasting, and for making sandwiches.

Yield: 1 large loaf, 12 to 14 slices

1 teaspoon Fleischmann's RapidRise Yeast (measured out from enclosed envelope)

Cornmeal-seed mixture for garnish (from the enclosed bag)

1 jar Going with the Grain Mix

Scant 2 cups ice water (add ice cubes to cold water and stir for 30 seconds before measuring), plus more if needed

About 1½ tablespoons corn oil, canola oil, or other flavorless oil for coating pan and dough top

FIRST RISE: Remove the yeast envelope and cornmeal-seed package (used for garnish) from the jar. In a large bowl, thoroughly stir together the jar of mix and 1 teaspoon of the yeast. Vigorously stir the ice water into the dry mix, scraping down the bowl sides and stirring until completely blended. If the dough is too dry to mix, gradually stir in just enough more ice water to blend the mixture; the dough should be stiff. Brush the top with a little oil. Tightly cover the bowl with plastic wrap. If desired, for best flavor or for convenience, refrigerate for 3 to 10 hours. Then let rise at cool room temperature (about 70°F) for 12 to 18 hours.

SECOND RISE: Generously oil a 9 × 5-inch loaf pan. Sprinkle half the cornmeal-seed mixture into the pan. Stir the dough briefly. With an oiled rubber spatula, scrape the dough in towards the center, working all the way around the bowl. Invert the dough into the pan. Brush the top lightly with oil, then smooth out and press into the pan with oiled fingertips. Brush the top generously with water, and immediately sprinkle the remaining cornmeal-seed mixture over the top. Cut a ½-inch-deep slash down the dough center using oiled kitchen shears or serrated knife. Cover the pan with nonstick spray-coated plastic wrap.

LET RISE USING EITHER OF THESE METHODS: For a 2- to 4-hour regular rise, let stand at warm (74° to 75°F) room temperature; or, for a 45-minute to 2-hour accelerated rise, let stand in a turned-off microwave along with 1 cup of boiling hot water. When the dough nears the plastic, remove it and continue the rise until the dough extends ½ inch above the pan rim.

BAKING PRELIMINARIES: 15 minutes before baking time, put a rack in the lower third of the oven; preheat to 450°F. Set the broiler pan on the oven floor.

BAKING: Reduce the heat to 425°F. Add a cup of water to the broiler pan, being careful of splattering and steam; don't refill if it boils dry. Bake on the lower rack for 35 to 45 minutes, or until the loaf is nicely browned. Cover the top with foil and continue baking for 20 to 25 minutes, until a skewer inserted in the thickest part comes out with just slightly moist particles clinging to the bottom portion (or until the center registers 204° to 207°F on an instant-read thermometer). Bake for 5 minutes more to ensure the center is fully done. Remove the loaf to the rack and cool completely.

SERVING AND STORING: The loaf slices best when cool, but is good served warm or at room temperature. Cool completely before storing. To maintain the crisp crust, store wrapped in a clean kitchen towel. Or store airtight in a plastic bag or wrapped in foil; this will prevent the loaf from drying out, but will cause the crust to soften. Store at room temperature for 3 days; freeze, airtight, for up to 2 months, then thaw, unwrapped, at room temperature. When thawed, re-crisp in a 375°F oven for a few minutes, if desired.

pull-apart
butter-top rolls

KS QUOTIENT—Fairly Easy: Easily assembled ingredients; two-stage mixing. Simple hand-shaping required.

The mild aroma, mellow taste, and melting texture of these home-style rolls remind me of ones that were the pride of the gray-haired ladies who baked for the frequent fund-raising church suppers my family attended during my childhood. Neatly aproned and hair-netted, they would stand in the back of the parish kitchen deftly turning out dozens of sheet pans of rolls, which were whisked straight from the ovens and devoured by eager tables of diners. For me (and probably for many other patrons) the highlight was not the featured ham or oysters or turkey, but those amazing all-you-could-eat butter rolls!

These rolls are made using the same dough as the County Fair White Bread (page 22). The very easy shortcut shaping method is one I borrowed from the church supper roll bakers, who used it because they had to produce huge quantities very quickly. It involves merely forming portions of dough into long logs and then cutting them crosswise into plump rectangles, so it's handy for inexperienced or very busy cooks as well. The rolls always expand and join together again during rising and baking, but, as their name suggests, they neatly pull apart when served.

Prepare the County Fair White Bread recipe up to the point it would normally be put into a loaf pan for the second rise; be sure to add the butter, milk powder, and egg as directed before proceeding with the following steps. (Note that the 1 tablespoon of egg reserved to glaze the loaf is not needed for the rolls.)

Yield: 24 finger rolls

1 recipe County Fair White Bread dough (see page 22), ready for the second rise

2 tablespoons unsalted butter, melted and slightly cooled

Unbleached white bread flour or all-purpose white flour for dusting

SECOND RISE: Coat a 9 × 13-inch baking dish or pan with nonstick spray. Coat a large sheet of baking parchment with nonstick spray, then dust with flour. Coat a very large cutting board with nonstick spray, then generously dust with flour.

Working in the bowl, generously dust the dough with flour, turning it until lightly coated all over. Smooth and press the flour into the dough until it is less sticky and easier to handle. Using well-oiled kitchen shears, divide the dough into thirds, placing each portion cut-side down and well separated on the parchment.

Working on the cutting board, press and pat one portion out into about a 5 × 10-inch rectangle, dusting with flour as needed to prevent stickiness. If the dough is resistant and springs back, let it rest for a few minutes, then continue. Tightly roll up the rectangle from the 10-inch side, forming a log. Pinch the seam tightly closed along the length of the log. Dust with more flour, then turn seam-side down. Stretch the log out from the middle until evenly thick and about 12 inches long, then flatten the log until it's about 2½ inches wide.

Using well-oiled kitchen shears or a large serrated knife, cut the log crosswise into 8 equal slices. Pat the row of rolls back into the log shape, then use a wide spatula to transfer them to the baking pan, placing the row lengthwise in the pan. Pull the rolls apart slightly so they fill the 13-inch length. Repeat the shaping and cutting process, laying the second and third log of rolls so they completely cover the pan; the rows will come together and fill it as they rise and bake. Brush the roll tops with half the butter. Tent the pan with nonstick spray-coated foil.

LET RISE USING ANY OF THESE METHODS: For a 1½- to 2½-hour regular rise, let stand at warm room temperature; for a 1- to 2-hour accelerated rise, let stand in a turned-off microwave along with 1 cup of boiling-hot water; or for an extended rise, refrigerate for 4 to 48 hours, then set out at room temperature. Continue the rise until the rolls double from their original size, removing the foil if the dough nears it.

BAKING PRELIMINARIES: 15 minutes before baking time, place a rack in the lower third of the oven; preheat to 350°F.

BAKING: Bake on the lower rack for 20 to 25 minutes, until the roll tops are nicely browned. Then cover with foil and bake for 3 to 5 minutes more or until a skewer inserted in the thickest part comes out with just a few particles clinging to the bottom (or until a center roll registers 204° to 206°F on an instant-read thermometer), to be sure the center is done. Brush the rolls with the remaining butter. Cool on a wire rack for 10 minutes. Lift the rolls from the pan and serve immediately.

SERVING AND STORING: Best served warm; reheat wrapped in foil in a preheated 350°F oven if desired. Cool thoroughly before storing. Store airtight in plastic or aluminum foil. The rolls will keep at room temperature for 2 to 3 days, and may be frozen, airtight, for up to 2 months.

COUNTY FAIR WHITE BREAD

Unlike the fluffy-stuff loaves lining supermarket shelves, this traditional enriched white bread has substance and texture and a buttery, yeasty smell. This is reminiscent of the loaves that often won the white bread category at the local county fairs when I was a child. True, it's not the sort of loaf that cutting-edge shops are selling these days, but when you want comfort food, or maybe a taste of home, this is it.

Yield: 1 large loaf, 12 to 14 slices

3 cups (15 ounces) unbleached white bread flour, plus ⅔ cup (3.33 ounces) or as needed

2½ tablespoons granulated sugar

1½ teaspoons table salt

¾ teaspoon Fleischmann's RapidRise Yeast

1¾ cups ice water, plus more if needed

3 tablespoons unsalted butter, melted and slightly cooled, plus extra for coating dough top and baking pan

¼ cup good-quality instant nonfat dry milk (don't use a generic brand)

1 large egg, at room temperature and beaten with a fork

FIRST RISE: In a large bowl, thoroughly stir together 3 cups of the flour, the sugar, salt, and yeast. Thoroughly stir the water into the bowl, scraping down the sides and mixing just until the ingredients are thoroughly blended. If the mixture is too dry to incorporate all the flour, a bit at a time, stir in enough more water to blend the ingredients and produce a fairly soft dough. Brush the top with butter. Cover the bowl with plastic wrap. If desired, for best flavor or for convenience, you can refrigerate the dough for 3 to 10 hours. Then, let rise at cool room temperature for 16 to 20 hours; if convenient, vigorously stir the dough about halfway through the rise.

SECOND RISE: In a medium bowl, stir together the butter, milk powder, and 2 tablespoons of the beaten egg until thoroughly blended; reserve the remaining egg for glazing the loaf top. Vigorously stir (or beat on low speed with a heavy-duty mixer with a dough hook) the butter mixture into the dough until smoothly and evenly incorporated; this may take several minutes. Gradually mix in ⅔ cup or enough more flour to yield a very hard-to-stir dough. Using a well-oiled rubber spatula, fold the dough in towards the center, working all the way around the bowl; this helps organize the gluten for shaping into a loaf.

Invert the dough into a well-greased 9 × 5-inch loaf pan. Smooth out the top and press evenly into the pan using a well-buttered rubber spatula or fingertips. Evenly brush the loaf top with the reserved beaten egg; don't allow the egg to pool around the pan edges, as it will cause sticking. Using well-buttered kitchen shears or a serrated knife, make a ½-inch-deep slash lengthwise down the center of the loaf. Cover the pan with nonstick spray-coated plastic wrap.

LET RISE USING ANY OF THESE METHODS: For a 1½- to 2½-hour regular rise, let stand at warm room temperature; for a 1- to 2-hour accelerated rise, let stand in a turned-off microwave along with 1 cup of boiling-hot water; or for an extended rise, refrigerate for 4 to 48 hours, then set out at room temperature. Continue the rise until the dough nears the plastic. Remove it and continue until the dough extends slightly above the pan rim.

BAKING PRELIMINARIES: 15 minutes before baking time, place a rack in the lower third of the oven; preheat to 375°F.

BAKING: Bake on the lower rack for 40 to 50 minutes, or until the top is nicely browned. Cover the top with foil and continue baking for 10 to 15 minutes longer, until a skewer inserted in the thickest part comes out with just a few particles clinging to the bottom (or until the center registers 208° to 210°F on an instant-read thermometer). Then bake for 5 to 10 minutes more to be sure the center is done. Cool in the pan on a wire rack for 10 minutes. Turn out the loaf onto the rack; cool thoroughly.

SERVING AND STORING: Cool thoroughly before slicing or storing. Store airtight in plastic or aluminum foil. The bread will keep at room temperature for 2 to 3 days, and may be frozen, airtight, for up to 2 months.

rosemary focaccia
with coarse salt

KS QUOTIENT — Easy: Few ingredients, easily mixed. Minimal hand-shaping

The name *focaccia* comes from the Latin *focus*, meaning "hearth," and this amazingly crusty flatbread was prepared long before modern-day ovens came on the scene. Especially in Italy, some versions are still baked on flat stones or tiles placed on coals, but for those without a hearth, a sheet pan set near the bottom of a hot, hot oven will do very well.

Puffy with hundreds of air pockets, crispy-chewy, and amazingly fragrant, focaccia makes the absolute most of simple ingredients like a little olive oil, coarse salt, and fresh rosemary. Don't even consider using the dried herb: Not only would its coarse, stick-like texture be intrusive, but during rehydration, it would draw too much moisture from the dough and discourage the formation of the gas bubbles essential for its enticing texture. This focaccia is so addictive, you may devour a portion of the pan even before it has had time to cool!

Yield: 12 to 15 servings

2¾ cups (13.75 ounces) unbleached all-purpose white flour, plus more as needed

2 tablespoons fresh rosemary needles (remove the stems), chopped fairly fine

¾ teaspoon table salt

1 teaspoon Fleischmann's RapidRise Yeast

1⅓ cups plus ½ teaspoon ice water, plus more as needed

2 tablespoons olive oil, divided, plus more as needed

¾ teaspoon sea salt or other coarse crystal salt

FIRST RISE: In a large bowl, thoroughly stir together the flour, rosemary, table salt, and yeast. Vigorously stir in the water, scraping down the bowl and mixing until the dough is thoroughly blended. Vigorously stir in 1 tablespoon of the olive oil. If the mixture is too dry to blend together, stir in just enough more ice water to facilitate mixing, but don't over-moisten, as the dough should be slightly stiff. If too wet, stir in enough more flour to firm it slightly. Evenly brush the top lightly with oil. Cover the bowl with plastic wrap. If desired, for best flavor or for convenience, you can refrigerate the dough for 3 to 10 hours. Then let rise at cool room temperature for 12 to 18 hours. If convenient, vigorously stir the dough partway through the rise.

SECOND RISE: Brush a 15 × 10 × 1-inch (or similar) baking pan with olive oil, then line the pan with baking parchment. Brush the parchment with olive oil. Using a well-oiled rubber spatula, turn the dough out onto the pan; try not to deflate it any more than necessary. Drizzle the dough with 1 tablespoon of olive oil. With well-oiled hands, lightly pat and press out the dough until it is evenly thick and extends to within 1 inch of the edges all around. Tent the pan with nonstick spray-coated plastic wrap.

LET RISE USING EITHER OF THESE METHODS: For a 2 ½- to 3½-hour regular rise, let stand at warm room temperature; or for an extended rise, refrigerate for 4 to 24 hours, then set out at room temperature. Continue the rise until the dough has almost doubled from the deflated size. (If the pan has a 1-inch rim, the dough should be ¼ inch below it.) Just before baking, with oiled fingertips, make deep indentations, or dimples, all over the dough. Sprinkle evenly with coarse salt.

BAKING PRELIMINARIES: 20 minutes before baking time, place a rack in lowest position in the oven; preheat to 500°F. Place the broiler pan on the oven floor.

BAKING: Reduce the temperature to 475°F. Add a cup of ice water to the broiler pan, being careful of splattering and steam. Bake on the lowest rack for 20 to 30 minutes, until golden brown, turning the pan from front to back for even browning about halfway through. Bake for 5 to 10 minutes more (or until the center registers 209° to 212°F on an instant-read thermometer) to be sure the center is done. Cool in the pan on a wire rack for 10 minutes. Using wide spatulas, lift the bread from the pan onto the rack to cool, or onto a cutting board to cut into servings.

SERVING AND STORING: Focaccia is best when fresh. Cut into rectangles and serve warm or at room temperature. Drizzle with additional olive oil or provide more as a dipping sauce, if desired. To maintain crispness, keep draped with a tea towel, at cool room temperature for 2 to 3 days. It may be frozen, airtight, for up to 2 months, but should be crisped in a preheated 400°F oven before serving.

VARIATION FENNEL SEED AND OREGANO (OR THYME) FOCACCIA WITH SALT—Prepare the dough exactly as for the rosemary version except omit the rosemary. When garnishing with the sea salt just before baking, also sprinkle the dough evenly with ½ teaspoon fennel seeds and ½ teaspoon dried oregano leaves or dried thyme leaves.

TIP: If you don't have fresh rosemary, try the fennel seed and oregano or thyme focaccia variation above. Don't add any more dried oregano or thyme than called for, because these herbs both have yeast-inhibiting chemicals that, in quantity, can discourage rising.

neapolitan-style
pizza dough

This is a simple, easy to handle, and virtually foolproof pizza dough calling for the most basic and economical supplies—yeast, salt, olive oil, and all-purpose flour. Some recipes call for a high-gluten flour, but I like regular flour better. The flat, thin layer doesn't need the extra gluten for support and the dough is more tender and much easier to stretch and shape without it. Because relatively little gluten development is necessary, the dough also requires less "micro-kneading" time than usual. After 4 to 12 hours on the countertop, it is ready to use, refrigerate, or freeze until needed.

The recipe makes enough dough for two 11- to 12-inch pizzas. If desired, freeze one or both dough portions for up to a month. Use *each* dough portion for one traditional tomato sauce and mozzarella pizza on the next page, or for another pizza of your own choosing.

Yield: Enough dough for two 11- to 12-inch pizzas

3 cups (15 ounces) unbleached all-purpose white flour, plus more as needed

Generous 1¼ teaspoons table salt

½ teaspoon Fleischmann's RapidRise Yeast

Scant 1½ cups ice water, plus more if needed

1 tablespoon olive oil, plus more for brushing over dough and pans

FIRST RISE: In a large bowl, thoroughly stir together the flour, salt, and yeast. Vigorously stir in the water, scraping down the sides, just until thoroughly blended. Stir in the olive oil until evenly incorporated. If the mixture is too dry to mix, add in just enough water to facilitate mixing, as the dough should be firm. If the dough is soft, stir in enough more flour to firm it. Brush the top with olive oil. Cover the bowl with plastic wrap. If desired, for best flavor or for convenience, you can refrigerate the dough for 3 to 10 hours. Then let rise at cool room temperature for 4 to 12 hours.

SECOND RISE: Stir the dough to deflate it. Divide it in half using oiled kitchen shears. The dough portions can be used immediately; or refrigerated for up to 12 hours and then used; or frozen, wrapped airtight, for up to 1 month. Use each half to prepare one pizza, following the recipe below.

TOMATO SAUCE AND MOZZARELLA PIZZA

Note that the recipe is designed so you can ready your pizza on a 12-inch pizza pan or a sheet of baking parchment. The dough, along with its pan or parchment, is then slipped onto a preheated baking sheet set on the lowest rack of the oven. This crisps the crust and eliminates any chance of sogginess, yet obviates the need for a pizza stone or baking tiles. (It's fine to use them if you have them, of course.) Once the dough is puffed and partly baked, add the toppings, then slip the pie back into the oven for its final turn. The result will assure your reputation as a first-rate pizza maker.

Yield: One 11½- to 12-inch pizza

½ recipe Neapolitan-Style Pizza Dough (see above), ready for the second rise

¾ cup homemade or store-bought tomato-based pizza sauce, at room temperature

¼ cup coarsely sliced (pitted) black Kalamata, Nicoise, or other flavorful brined black olives, optional

4 to 6 ounces fresh mozzarella cheese, thinly sliced

SECOND RISE: Place the dough portion on a 12-inch lightly oiled pizza pan or a large sheet of nonstick spray–coated baking parchment. Drizzle lightly with olive oil, then press and stretch the dough into an 11½- to 12-inch round with oiled fingertips; if it is resistant and springs back, let it rest for a few minutes before continuing. The shape doesn't have to be perfect, but be sure to push the dough outward to slightly build up and thicken the edges (which would burn if too thin). Set aside to rise, tented with nonstick spray–coated foil, for 25 to 45 minutes, depending on whether you prefer a thin, slightly dense crust, or a lighter, medium-thick one.

BAKING PRELIMINARIES: 20 minutes before baking time, place a rack in the lowest slot of the oven; preheat to 500°F. Place a rimless baking sheet (or place a rimmed sheet upside down) on the lowest rack.

BAKING: Place the pizza pan with the dough (or the dough on the parchment) on the preheated baking sheet. Bake for 7 to 10 minutes, or until the dough begins to firm and puff up. Remove from the oven and spread the sauce to within ⅓ inch of the edge all around. Add the olives, if using, and the mozzarella slices evenly over the top. Return to the oven and bake until the top is bubbly and the edge is puffy and nicely browned, about 10 minutes longer. Transfer the pan to a wire rack and cool for 5 minutes before serving.

SERVING AND STORING: Serve hot; cut into wedges with kitchen shears or a pizza wheel. Reheat, wrapped in foil, in a 350°F oven for 5 to 10 minutes or under a microwave-safe plastic cover on medium power for a minute or so. Store airtight and refrigerated for 2 to 3 days, or frozen, airtight, for up to a week. Thaw before reheating.

simple streusel
coffeecake

KS QUOTIENT—Fairly Easy: Simple ingredients; easy mixing; make-ahead option. No hand-shaping.

This coffeecake truly is simplicity itself, yet it has a lovely buttery taste and texture that will ensure your reputation as a talented baker. The outside is wonderfully crisp-tender and strewn with a crunchy, nut-accented sugar-cinnamon streusel. The inside is moist, soft, and studded with more little nuggets of streusel. It is great warm from the oven, especially for breakfast, brunch, or a coffee klatch. The coffeecake can be baked and served in a flat 9 × 15-inch baking pan, or, for a fancier presentation, baked in an angel food pan, then lifted off and plated attractively.

The recipe is super-convenient because the streusel can be made well in advance and used to jazz up a coffeecake as needed. Better yet, the coffeecake can be completely assembled and refrigerated for up to 36 hours. By planning ahead, you can remove it from the refrigerator to warm up and rise (allow for a 4½- to 5-hour regular rise, or a 3- to 3½-hour accelerated rise) and time the baking to have a fresh, warm coffeecake coming from the oven just when you need it.

Don't forget that this recipe starts with a batch of All-Purpose Enriched Sweet Dough. All the first- and second-stage ingredients should be already incorporated into the dough when the following preparations begin.

Yield: 1 large coffeecake, 12 to 15 portions or slices

1 batch All-Purpose Enriched Sweet Dough, prepared as directed (see page 36) (adding the eggs, butter, etc., and maximum amount of sugar called for, then proceeding with preparing the coffeecake as follows)

1 batch Make-Ahead Streusel, prepared as directed (see page 38) (if just made, it should be refrigerated until firmed up slightly; if made ahead, it should be set out until warmed up just slightly but still firm)

SECOND RISE: Stir a generous half of the streusel into the batch of dough. For a shaped, round coffeecake, turn out the dough into a well-oiled or nonstick spray-coated 8- to 12-quart angel food pan. For a rectangular coffeecake, turn out the dough in a well-oiled 9 × 13-inch flat baking dish. Spread the dough out evenly using an oiled rubber spatula. Sprinkle the remaining streusel evenly over the dough. Cover the pan or baking dish with nonstick spray-coated plastic wrap.

LET RISE USING ANY OF THESE METHODS: For a 2- to 3-hour regular rise, let stand at warm room temperature; for a 1½- to 2½-hour accelerated rise, let stand in a turned-off microwave along with 1 cup of boiling-hot water; or for an extended rise, refrigerate for 4 to 36 hours, then set out at room temperature. If the dough nears the plastic wrap, remove it and continue the rise until the dough has doubled from its deflated size.

BAKING PRELIMINARIES: 15 minutes before baking time, place a rack in the lower third of the oven; preheat to 350°F.

BAKING: Bake on the lower rack for 30 to 40 minutes for the rectangular coffeecake or 40 to 50 minutes for the ring-shaped coffeecake, until the top is nicely browned and a skewer inserted in the thickest part comes out with only a few particles at the bottom end (or the center registers 205° to 207°F on an instant-read thermometer). If necessary, cover with foil for the last 15 to 20 minutes to prevent over-browning. Then bake for another 5 to 10 minutes to ensure the center is done. Cool in the pan on a wire rack for 15 minutes. If baked in an angel food pan, run a knife around the center tube and sides to loosen the loaf, then lift it up and onto the rack.

SERVING AND STORING: Serve the rectangular cake from its pan; serve the round version on a cake plate. The coffeecake slices best when cool, but is delicious warm. Cool completely before storing airtight in plastic or foil; or store the round coffeecake in a cake keeper. Keeps at room temperature for up to 3 days, and may be frozen, airtight, for up to 2 months.

ALL-PURPOSE ENRICHED SWEET DOUGH

This is a versatile, slightly sweet dough suitable for making coffee-cakes, various enriched loaves, and dessert breads. Since the dough can be put to different purposes, you can adjust the amount of sugar slightly to suit your taste. However, for proper gluten development and yeast growth, be sure to add the sugar in two stages, as directed, and don't add more than the maximum called for.

Yield: Enough dough for 1 generous loaf or coffeecake

2⅓ cups (11.66 ounces) unbleached all-purpose white flour, plus ⅔ cup (3.33 ounces) plus more as needed

5 to 7 tablespoons granulated sugar, to taste, divided

1¼ teaspoons table salt

1 teaspoon Fleischmann's RapidRise Yeast

1¼ cups ice water, plus more if needed

Flavorless vegetable oil for brushing

⅓ cup good-quality instant nonfat dry milk (do not use a generic brand)

6 tablespoons unsalted butter, melted and cooled just slightly

2 large eggs, at room temperature, beaten

FIRST RISE: In a large bowl, thoroughly stir together 2⅓ cups of the flour, 2 tablespoons of the sugar, the salt, and yeast. Vigorously stir in the water, scraping down the bowl and mixing until the dough is thoroughly blended. If the mixture is too dry to incorporate the flour, a bit at a time, mix in just enough more water to blend the ingredients. If the mixture is soft, stir in enough more

flour to make it firm, but not hard to stir. Evenly brush the top lightly with vegetable oil. Tightly cover the bowl with plastic wrap. If desired, for best flavor or for convenience, refrigerate for 3 to 4 hours. Then let rise at cool room temperature for 12 to 18 hours.

SECOND RISE: In a medium bowl, stir together the remaining 3 to 5 tablespoons of sugar, the milk powder, and butter, then mix in the eggs until well blended. Gradually add the egg mixture, then ⅔ cup flour, to the dough, mixing until evenly incorporated; this will take several minutes so it's best to use a dough hook and heavy-duty mixer on low, if possible. If necessary, add in enough more flour to yield a hard-to-stir dough, scraping down the bowl sides carefully. Proceed with the dough as directed in the coffee-cake recipe (see page 35).

MAKE-AHEAD STREUSEL

This is a simple, cinnamon-and-butter streusel mixture that can be stashed in the refrigerator and tossed together with a dough to create a great coffeecake almost instantly (see the Simple Streusel Coffee-cake recipe, page 34).

Yield: Enough for 1 large coffeecake

1 cup packed light brown sugar

¾ cup unbleached all-purpose white flour

2 teaspoons ground cinnamon

¼ teaspoon salt

½ cup (1 stick) unsalted butter, melted

⅔ cup chopped walnuts or pecans

In a medium bowl, thoroughly stir together the brown sugar, flour, cinnamon, and salt, breaking up any lumps of sugar as you work. Stir in the butter until evenly incorporated and the mixture forms small clumps. Stir in the nuts. Refrigerate until firmed up, about an hour. Just before using, break up any large clumps with fingertips or a pastry cutter. Use as directed in the coffeecake recipe. If not using immediately, refrigerate, airtight, for up to 3 weeks. Let warm up slightly before using.

great granola
breakfast bread

KS QUOTIENT — Easy: Easily assembled ingredients and easy preparation. No hand-shaping.

Enriched with both granola and milk, this large, slightly sweet loaf is great for breakfast on the go. It's also good for toasting and makes a fine French toast or brunch bread. The loaf has a handsome, nubby-crusty top and light crumb accented with pleasing little patches and bursts of granola flavor. It always receives compliments and is a favorite with my family and friends.

Almost any purchased or homemade granola you like will do for this recipe; I'm partial to honey-oat with almonds. Whatever your choice, if it's coarse and chunky, crush it into fine (⅛-inch) bits before using. The easiest way is to put it into a sturdy plastic bag and either squeeze and press it with your hands, or, if it's hard and crunchy, go over it with a rolling pin (or a wine bottle if that's handier!).

Makes 1 large loaf, 12 to 14 slices

3 cups (15 ounces) unbleached all-purpose white flour, plus more as needed

3 tablespoons granulated sugar, plus 1 tablespoon for garnish

1¼ teaspoons table salt

¾ teaspoon Fleischmann's RapidRise Yeast

1¼ cups plus 2 tablespoons ice water, plus more if needed

3 tablespoons corn oil, canola oil or other flavorless vegetable oil, plus more for dough top and pan

1⅓ cups plain, raisin, honey-oat, mixed fruit and nut, or other fine-textured granola, plus 4 tablespoons for garnish

⅓ cup top-quality instant nonfat powdered milk (don't use a generic brand)

FIRST RISE: In a large bowl, thoroughly stir together the flour, sugar, salt, and yeast. In another bowl or measuring cup, whisk together the water and oil. Vigorously stir the mixture into the bowl with the flour, scraping down the sides until the ingredients are thoroughly blended. If the mixture is too dry to incorporate all the flour, a bit at a time, stir in just enough more ice water to blend the ingredients; don't over-moisten, as the dough should be stiff. Brush or spray the top with oil. Cover the bowl with plastic wrap. If desired, for best flavor or for convenience, you can refrigerate the dough for 3 to 10 hours. Then let rise at cool room temperature for 12 to 18 hours.

SECOND RISE: Vigorously stir the dough, gradually sprinkling over the 1⅓ cups granola and the milk powder; continue stirring until evenly distributed throughout the dough. Very generously oil a 9 × 5-inch loaf pan. Sprinkle with 2 tablespoons of the granola and tip the pan back and forth to distribute it over the bottom and sides. Turn out the dough into the pan. Brush or spray the loaf top with oil. Using an oiled rubber spatula or your fingertips, smooth and press the dough evenly into the pan. Sprinkle the top with the remaining 2 tablespoons granola, pressing down lightly. Cover the bowl with nonstick spray-coated plastic wrap.

LET RISE USING ANY OF THESE METHODS: For a 2- to 3-hour regular rise, let stand at warm room temperature; for a 1- to 2-hour accelerated rise, let stand in a turned-off microwave along with 1 cup of boiling-hot water; or for an extended rise, refrigerate, covered, for 4 to 48 hours, then set out at room temperature. Continue the rise until the dough nears the plastic. Remove it and continue until the dough extends ¼ inch above the pan rim.

BAKING PRELIMINARIES: 15 minutes before baking time, place a rack in the lower third of the oven; preheat to 375°F. Sprinkle the loaf with the 1 tablespoon sugar.

BAKING: Bake on the lower rack for 40 to 50 minutes, until the top is nicely browned. Cover with foil and continue baking for 25 to 30 minutes, until a skewer inserted in the thickest part comes out with just a few crumbs on the tip (or until center registers 205° to 208°F on an instant-read thermometer). When the loaf seems done, bake for 5 minutes longer to ensure the center is baked through. Cool in the pan on a wire rack for 10 to 15 minutes. Remove the loaf to the rack. Cool thoroughly.

SERVING AND STORING: The loaf slices best when cool, but tastes good warm. Cool completely before storing airtight in plastic or foil. It will keep at room temperature for 2 to 3 days, and may be frozen, airtight, for up to 2 months.

Additional Tips for Success

To help you follow and carry out the recipe instructions, here are some additional details.

MEASURING FLOUR

Flour measurements for recipes in this book are made by dipping a measuring cup into a flour sack or canister, overfilling the dry measure slightly, then sweeping across its top with a long-bladed spatula or straight-edged knife to even the surface. Don't tap or shake the cup or try to compact the flour. Don't try to fluff it up.

Even careful measuring with the right cups will not yield the same quantity every time because the volume of flour is affected by other factors such as settling during production and shipping. Our recipes compensate for this by indicating what consistency the dough should be at key points. Feel free to add more flour or water as necessary to achieve the dough consistency indicated.

READYING ICE WATER

Each recipe calls for ice water. To achieve the correct temperature, fill a large measuring cup with the amount of water specified, then add a heaping cup of ice cubes and stir vigorously for 30 seconds. Finally, measure out the exact amount of water (discard the cubes) and incorporate it into the dry ingredients as directed. In most cases, tap water is satisfactory, but if yours is heavily chlorinated or unpleasant-tasting, try bottled water and see if your breads are noticeably tastier.

SPRITZING (OR BRUSHING) AND COVERING THE DOUGH

Each recipe calls for brushing or spritzing dough with oil (or perhaps butter) to prevent the surface from drying out during the rising period. The easiest method is to use nonstick spray; be sure to use a high-quality brand with corn oil or other neutral-flavored oil. Or, if preferred, simply brush the dough surface evenly with a little corn oil using a pastry brush, rubber scraper, or your fingertips. To further prevent surface drying, cover the bowl with plastic wrap. As a precaution against the dough sticking to the plastic, also spray the plastic with nonstick cooking spray.

ESTIMATING RISING TIMES AND CHOOSING A RISING METHOD

The yeast are living organisms, so their growth rate depends on the temperature of the dough and the room. As a result, the rise times given in the recipes are guidelines only. If your room is much warmer than normal, check the dough sooner than indicated. If the room is much colder, expect the dough to rise more slowly. If you live at a high altitude, expect it to rise 25 to 50 percent faster than normal.

While the first rise needs to be cool and unhurried for good bread flavor and texture, it's fine to speed up or slow down the second rise to suit your schedule by selecting an "accelerated" rise or an "extended" refrigerator rise.

Accelerated Rise (for the second rise only):

An accelerated rise can reduce the second rise time by a third to a half. Bring a 1-cup glass measure of tap water to a boil in a microwave oven. Let the cup stand a minute or two, then set in corner of the microwave. Set the dough (in its baking pan and covered) inside and close the door. If dough is not sufficiently risen after an hour or so in the microwave, temporarily remove the dough, and bring the water to a boil again to provide a second burst of warmth for the yeast.

Extended Rise (for the second rise):

The extended refrigerator rise method lets you put off baking for up to two days by storing the dough in the refrigerator. When you're ready to "restart" the rise, let the dough stand on the counter until it returns to room temperature (usually 1½ to 2 hours), then proceed with a regular or accelerated rise. Note that holding a dough longer than 48 hours can result in a denser baked good.

How to Know When the Dough Has Risen Enough:

Each recipe suggests how high the dough should rise in the pan before baking. Some doughs do much of their rising after they're in the oven, others rise very little during baking. To know if the dough is ready for baking, press a finger into the dough: If the indention stays instead of filling up again, the dough is sufficiently raised and ready for baking. If a loaf rises *significantly* more than it should, stir it down, return it to the pan, and let it rise again (over-raised doughs tend to sink or collapse during baking).

TESTING FOR DONENESS

Rapping a loaf on top or observing crust color is never sufficient for judging doneness. The most foolproof way is to use a thermometer and bake to the degree specified in the recipe. Or, insert a skewer or thin knife into the center then withdraw it; if the crumbs on the tip look wet or gooey, continue baking until they look dry and slightly crumbly. Then bake an extra 5 to 10 minutes to be sure the center is fully done. When in doubt, err on the side of over-baking. If the outside begins to over-brown, cover it with foil.

STORING BREADS

Start by putting freshly baked breads on a rack and cooling them thoroughly before storing. Soft breads should be stored in an airtight plastic bag or container. Crusty breads should be placed in a paper or cloth bag, or wrapped in a kitchen towel. Each recipe provides storage instructions based on whether the bread needs to stay crisp or soft. Once stored, loaves will keep in a cool, dry spot (not refrigerated) for up to three days. Refrigeration will speed staling of the bread.

To keep a bread longer than three days, freeze it in a heavy, airtight plastic freezer bag for up to two months. Some staling may occur but it can be mostly reversed by wrapping the thawed bread loosely in foil and reheating it at 400°F for 15 to 20 minutes. Refresh individual slices or rolls by wrapping them in a towel and microwaving them on 50 percent power for around 30 seconds; use immediately.

Recipe Index